A FREE ONLINE COMMUNITY FOR BOOK LOVERS.

## Contributors

Efren O'Brien
Jude Austin
Charles Townsend
Michael Hegarty
Peter S. Rush
Susan Smith Jones, PhD
E. Alan Fleischauer
Anthony A. Morris
Dan E. Hendrickson
Londyn Skye
Onyx Gold
Mike L Junior
Peter S. Rush
Ron Tripodo
Ken Rusk
Charlie Sheldon
Fred G. Baker
Garon Whited
Jude Austin
N.L. Holmes
Rob White
Martin Kendall
Gary Robinson
Jack Winnick
Van Fleisher
Dr.Ghoulem Berrah
Pejay Bradley
Noel Hankin
Werner Neff

Founder and Creator of OnlineBookClub: Scott
Hughes
Director & Editor-in-Chief: S. Jeyran Main
Publisher: Onlinebookclub.org
Print & Distribution: IngramSpark
ISBN 978-1-988680-26-2 (Paperback)
ISBN 978-1-988680-27-9 (Digital)
onlinebookclub.org
For all inquiries, please contact:
magazine@onlinebookclub.org

# Table of Contents

# EDITOR'S NOTE

Happy New Year and Happy Holidays to all our readers. There is an existential moment with the whole new year "thing." It brings a lot of reflection and hope leading up to and after January. While I appreciate the inspiration igniting a fresh start to the year, I always wonder how the "new" becomes an antidote to all that was wrong with the "old" and why we would view it this way.

Could this be us wanting to be hopeful for the anticipation ignited by the prospect of the "new" being misplaced by all the "old" that used to be good and made us happy? Have we lost all the familiar and comfortable feelings we used to have in the past and unknowingly replaced them with the now unfamiliar and little painful ones? Could we just be trying to restore what has been lost? Food for thought.

We welcome the magazine's second edition with author confessions and words of wisdom from the writing community. The importance of writing about what you want is discussed, and how following your heart can influence what you ultimately publish becomes inevitable. We also introduce a few "how-to's" in plotting your book or getting started as a writer.

Thank you for the support and all the contributors who have made this issue happen. The writing community has never failed, proving its strength and passion towards platforms such as this one.

Here's to happy comings!

*Jeyran Main*

Director & Editor-in-chief
OnlineBookClub Magazine

## CONFESSIONS OF A "CLOSET" HISTORY BUFF

**EFREN O'BRIEN**

It's thought of as nerdy to be a History Buff. It's not really "kool." We are so focused on the "here and now!" Also, we live in times where we are more focused on "self" than ever before. We have more distractions daily that disrupt our work than ever before.

We don't take time to contemplate life, the lives of generations before us, or what they were really like as people. But those questions and thoughts have been part of my makeup for years. It convinced me to write Historical Fiction and incorporate my own characters into actual historical scenarios.

I was living in Santa Fe, New Mexico, and I wanted to write Historical Fiction but wasn't exactly sure what to write about. After all, there is enough History surrounding Santa Fe to fill several hundred normal-sized novels. The city is a museum itself. I wasn't really interested in the development of the city. Still, when I heard that the Confederate Army had actually occupied Santa Fe in 1862, during the Civil War... that piqued my interest, and I wanted to learn more. So I researched and found out that about 3,300 rambunctious Texans had crossed the desert of West Texas in the Fall of 1861 and traveled north up the Rio Grande River all the way to Santa Fe. And at that point, I was hooked. I've always been interested in the US Civil War. What were the people like then? How did they live? How was that war actually fought? Those questions drove me to develop my own characters and study two fascinating Civil War battles actually fought in New Mexico, The Battle of Valverde Ford and the Battle of Glorieta Pass. The in-depth research paid off when my novel, "The Deserving," was published in October 2017. I invite you to read my book. I think you'll find it an enjoyable story, and I'm confident you'll learn about the Civil War in the West and life at that time that you didn't know about before! Happy Reading!

# THE IMPORTANCE OF WRITING WHAT YOU WANT

## JUDE AUSTIN

The worst day of my writing career was when my novel, Tsunami, was published.

The best day was when the publisher confirmed it was entirely out of print and agreed to give me the ebook rights so I could ensure it would never again see the light of day.

I hate it. I hated it all the time I was writing it, and I would give any amount of money to be able to unwrite it. Tsunami was a book I was essentially coerced into writing because a family member told me that nobody was interested in sci-fi. So I'd have to write a different genre if I wanted to get anywhere. I was 22 and had already completed three sci-fi/fantasy novels (Danshi, Kheshen and Tulor). I'd found my niche but was still young enough to think that this person knew better about what I should be writing than I did.

They did not. Although not a bad novel in itself, even I could tell that Tsunami was nowhere near my usual level, to the point where one of my readers was surprised to hear it was published in 2006 and cited my earlier work on Fanfiction.net (around 2002) as being of a far higher standard.

It was a hard lesson but very well learned. You know your genre. You know your strengths better than anyone. Going outside your comfort zone is great and helps you to grow as a writer, but only if you do it for the right reasons. There's a huge difference between choosing to step outside your comfort zone and letting yourself be dragged out of it; the readers will know the difference. More importantly, so will you.

# HOW I PLOTTED MY BOOKS

**CHARLES TOWNSEND**

Before I wrote "The Magician's Secret," I decided I wanted to write a book that got the reader always wanting to know what happened next. When a story is told from several points of view, I believe it slows the story down every time it swaps from one to another. I, therefore, decided to make it from just a single point of view, that of the protagonist.

I also wanted the plot to have plenty of twists and to paint a picture in the reader's mind of what was going on. Finally, I tried to devise characters who would interact well together.

The first stage in producing the book's actual plot was to outline where I wanted the book to go. I then broke it down into stages or steps that needed to be gone through to reach the end conclusion. At this point, I had not worked out how these steps would be achieved.

Then I started to write. Before starting each stage, I thought about how that stage could be achieved. I then chose the one that seemed the most fun. These stages roughly corresponded with the book's chapters.

This method meant that the book tended to become a series of episodes. Many reviewers have said the books are very cinematic and would make a good film or TV series; in fact, each book would easily break down into six episodes.

Once I had worked out how a stage would go, I wrote it very fast. I have a good visual imagination; I visualized what was happening and then described what I saw. I tried letting the characters tell the story with dialogue as much as possible.

The books make up the "Illusions of Power" trilogy. They are "The Magician's Secret," The Three Card Trick," and "The Magic Lantern." Each book was written to be able to stand on its own as well as be part of the trilogy.

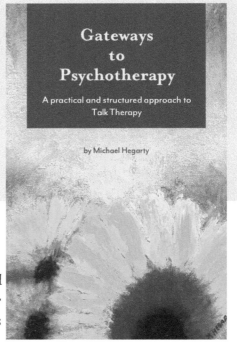

# BIRTH AND DEATH AND IN BETWEEN

### MICHAEL HEGARTY

Brenda, my partner, and I both had been diagnosed with terminal cancer in the same week in December 2020, though the paths of our illnesses soon went in very different directions. Brenda's cancer was of the kidney variety, and she started chemotherapy immediately.

The immediate challenge that came to me was writing a book with a brief account of my personal journey and leaving a legacy to my healing therapy profession. Brenda backed me all the way.

I have a friend who had written and published several books before me. I told him that I had just finished the script of my first book, with a self-satisfied look of achievement on my face.

He said, "That's fantastic, Mike. Congratulations."

He asked me, "Have you had any colleagues review it?" No.

"Have you asked other professionals in your field to critique it?" No.

"Have you spoken to publishers?" No.

Then he said, "Sorry to tell you; you're just starting the process."

It took 6 months and 11 more drafts to get the first edition printed.

I learned that, in Ireland, we have a very high proportion of writers and readers. When I sought bookstores to take my book, significant outlets had contracts with the big publishers, and the "Bestsellers" shelves held their books to the exclusion of independent writers.

I dedicated my book "Gateways to Psychotherapy" to Brenda, and we both launched the book in Galway City in the West of Ireland on the 14th of June, 2022. We enjoyed our days and nights and our holiday breaks in those last days. She went through many, many hospital oncology stays. Exactly 2 months after my book was launched, my beautiful Brenda (aged 54) passed away at home surrounded by those she loved. I continue to promote my book and live my life with Brenda's wonderful and positive encouragement ringing in my ears.

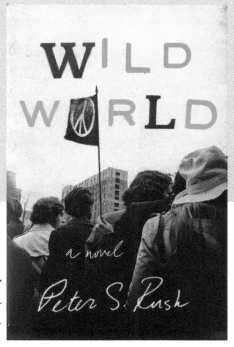

# WORDS OF WISDOM

## PETER S. RUSH

I have been a professional writer for many years as a newspaper reporter, magazine writer, and editor. My first book was non-fiction. Because of my background, I found non-fiction fairly-straight forward.

You must do your research, confirm your facts, check your sources, cite your references, and find a hook for the story. After assembling all the information, I create an outline for the story to ensure I can keep the facts straight. I find the writing process to be linear in nature. I am very much a planner.

When I began writing my first novel, I found that my non-fiction process did not work for me. Fiction involves people with lives, thoughts, feelings, and unique persona. My approach is episodic in nature, as I can now define it. I take the story and write as much as possible in the first draft, not caring if all the pieces fit together. My process entails rewriting, in which I try to sculpt my characters into people.

My thought process is in scenes – the scenes that make up the lives of these characters. I must allow each character to have a voice I can recognize. I like to feel my surroundings, smell the aromas, hear the noises and touch the surfaces. My work to date is historical fiction – but recent history, not centuries ago. It is a messy process because it is how I feel comfortable creating it. I don't believe life is predictable, so neither should my stories or characters. I generally have an idea of the arch of the story, but sometimes my characters surprise me by taking unexpected turns. When they do, I go with them to see where it turns out. I hope some of the characters are truly memorable. I admit I've written some excellent scenes that were cut before the final manuscript was finished. I believe stories are all around us; a good writer will make them compelling.

# DREAM BIG & FOLLOW YOUR HEART: HOW I GOT STARTED AS A WRITER

## SUSAN SMITH JONES, PHD

As I travel the world giving talks and doing media interviews, I am often asked: "Susan, you are such a prolific writer, and your healthy living and lifestyle books are in multiple languages worldwide. How did you first get interested in writing?"

Books have always been my friends. In my childhood bedroom, I devoted a special corner to my own personal library with beautiful books in full color that occupied my days and nights and always kept me company. I put some of my favorite passages from books on beautiful paper, decorating these pages with lots of colors, and then taped them to the ceiling of my bedroom so when I went to sleep, I could look up at the enchanting words.

I never felt alone growing up because reading gave me such joy and comfort, and imagination with no limits. Reading always inspired, motivated, and empowered me. Through reading all kinds of books, from the classics to nonfiction and fiction, to travel guides and poetry, I could triumphantly journey in my mind to any place in the world—far and wide—without the slightest bit of limitation or hesitation. Copious reading expanded my imagination, and I learned to visualize the books' characters and put myself into the role of the heroines. Often in parts of fiction books, I would read and think about ways to write it better or change the plot to a more fantastical or exhilarating storyline that worked better for my mindset. This practice came in handy for me during countless hours of babysitting when I made up stories to recite to the children.

Instead of my parents and grandparents reading to me as a young girl, I almost always insisted on reading the books to them. Sometimes during these readings, I would stop and explain to them what the words meant to me. My family enjoyed lots of chuckles with my penchant for reading and books. Words, and pages with words that had meaning, resonated in my heart as a young girl and still do to this day. The fact that letters are made into words, and words are made into sentences, and sentences made into paragraphs can create all kinds of emotions and deeply touch the heart, and literally help to transform lives and make the world a better place to live is astonishing and so powerful to me. Through reading, we can feel happy, sad, positive, hopeful, joyous, upset, blissful, anxious, energized, invigorated, stimulated, vitalized, elated, and so much more. And this is how I started in the magnificent world of writing books. Loving to read as a child parlayed into loving to write as an adult.

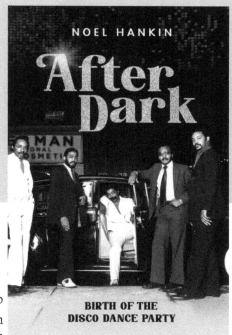

**BIRTH OF THE
DISCO DANCE PARTY**

# WHY I WROTE A BOOK

**NOEL HANKIN**

In 1971, I was part of a group of young men who formed a social club called The Best of Friends. We created social events in midtown Manhattan that attracted diverse patrons: rich and poor, black and white, gay and straight.

These events featured new, hi-fidelity sound systems, upbeat music that made you want to dance, the glitz and glamor of ever-changing lights, and innovative DJing techniques. The admission price was low, so almost anyone could attend. The experience we created was fresh and enabled a level of human interaction and acceptance that was unprecedented.

Many patrons of those early discotheques remember that period as the best in their lives, and they want future generations to know about it. We all hoped a skilled writer would take on this task, but no one stepped up. I am not a writer, but I know how to tell a story. So, during the Covid pandemic, I wrote After Dark: Birth of the Disco Dance Party.

Discos existed before 1971, such as the Peppermint Lounge and the Cheetah, but they did not ignite the craze. The craze started in black and gay clubs in New York City. Gay clubs were somewhat insulated because few had proper licensing, so they were underground. Some gay clubs did not welcome women. In contrast, our five discotheques welcomed all with equal enthusiasm and were fully licensed. Leviticus, Justine's, and Bogard's were among the first black-owned clubs in midtown Manhattan. We also owned Lucifer's in Queens and Brandi's in Brooklyn. Our clubs paved the way for Saturday Night Fever and Studio 54, debuting in 1977.

TBOF created something special that, along with a few other clubs in New York, contributed significantly to a new way to socialize and interact with one another. Our discotheques were compelling and inclusive — everyone felt welcomed. No purely social occasion had greater diversity. The popularity of these dance parties swept across the country like a tidal wave. That tidal wave was disco.

# THE FOUNDING FATHERS

**WERNER NEFF**

The United States was founded in the late 18th century as the first republic based on modern democratic rules. The texts of The Constitution and The Bill of Rights dominated the country's ruling with the separation of powers to legislature, executive, and judiciary.

What the Founding Fathers learned from the Greeks and Romans shaped this country. America created the model for modern democracy, later copied by countries worldwide.

Today, we are struggling to maintain democracy as it was designed, and we are drifting into an erosion of those principles—thus enabling and tolerating inequality, poverty, helplessness, and mistrust. A distortion of our democracy is the covert voting restrictions and gerrymandering, calling forth a hidden betrayal of the American people.

In this book, the author reflects on history, politics, democratic theories, and principles in the form of fictional dialogs allowing the Founding Fathers to express their theories on what truly makes America great and what will provide the American people today with real freedom and prosperity. The author believes that democratic principles and ethical and selfless leadership in service of the people are the pillars of justice, equality, and prosperity for all.

You might be interested in meeting the Founding Fathers these days...

## Reconfigurement: Reconfiguring Your Life at Any Stage and Planning Ahead

### E. Alan Fleischauer

Did you know that an essential aspect of financial planning is making finances? It is, and E. Alan Fleischauer authored Reconfigurement to disclose such fundamental but subtle truths and many more that we do not often think about. The author has been a financial advisor for over 20 years and wrote this book to bridge the great divide between reality and tradition. It behooves us to find newer strategies as we live longer but still rely on principles established to serve generations with shorter life expectancies primarily.

We are standing at a crossroads where people are torn between spending what they have and later relying solely on meager pension payments or making extra plans for retirement for the inevitabilities of life. What is undeniable is, owing to development and improvements in various spheres of life, life expectancy has increased tremendously. Fleischauer states, "Reconfigurement financial planning is a turning point." This turning point is the foundation of the paradigm shift in how we view retirement, starting with solutions that appeal to both the right and left centers of the brain.

A good self-help book does not require understanding rocket science to apply its principles and concepts. One of the signs that this was one of the best books I had ever read on financial planning and management and making career decisions was that I could undergo some of the assessments and get pragmatic results. I am already adding the skills I got from the tests to my resume and LinkedIn profile. This book will help you reconfigure your career life to suit your personality, passion, and work style.

From busting prevailing myths, including myths and misconceptions surrounding Social Security and the Social Security Administration, to providing advice on healthy aging, Fleischauer leaves nothing to chance. The reader will also enjoy the jokes in every chapter as they enhance the reading experience. Overall, I disliked nothing about the book. Consequently, I rate it 4 out of 4 stars.

Aging is something that everyone who has been born goes through. Old age will eventually knock, and the best way to prepare for this stage is to read this book, understand its concepts, and apply some of the lessons. I am glad the author did not advise readers to eliminate their tax and financial advisors. You will still work with them, but you will be better equipped to make informed, evidence-based decisions.

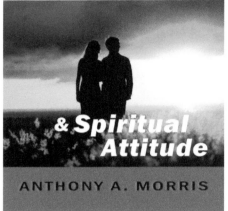

*Understand & overcome the ancient secrets interfering with your **sexual & spiritual joy***

# Good Sexual Hygiene & Spiritual Attitude: Human Ethics

## Anthony A. Morris

Our mind is powerful, and we can drastically improve our lives by changing our thoughts. Thus, the more a particular thought or belief is activated and reinforced, the more it becomes a way we do things. This is all that Anthony A. Morris tries to teach us in this book.

Anthony A. Morris, in Good Sexual Hygiene & Spiritual Attitude, tries to educate parents and adults on how to answer or give replies to questions asked by a child or their children. He focuses on questions about sex and anything relating to life. The author warned that lies should not be told to these children in any way, or it might affect them later in life. He says that we should explore our spiritual attitude.

This means researching and putting in personal effort rather than listening to someone dictate what the Holy Bible says. He believes that many people are brainwashed through fear into total subservience by their spiritual leaders or Churches. He tries to inspire his readers to think for themselves.

This book has a lot of positive aspects. I like that the author seems genuinely concerned for youth. His tone can be read to be very concerned about youth development. The author relates what he says to true events that happened to him. Through these events, I got a clearer understanding of the information he was trying to pass along. He also wants to teach youth and adults how to think for themselves. He mentions that the youth should not follow the crowd. This valuable lesson is important even to a person like me.

I only came across things I liked in this book. I am thrilled I came across it. The book's cover caught my attention, and its content kept me intrigued from start to finish.

This book was also exceptionally written and remarkably well edited because I did not encounter any grammatical or typographical errors. This book is a 4 out of 4 because it has all the elements of an amazing book. This book has some religious content because many verses in the Bible were quoted, and many topics were compared with the teachings from the Bible.

This book is first and foremost recommended to people who are planning to have kids or already have children. I also recommend this book to adults and young adults alike because it improves our thinking and how we see life. This book definitely makes an amazing read for an interested reader.

# Brandy Ballad of a Pirate Princes

## Dan E. Hendrickson

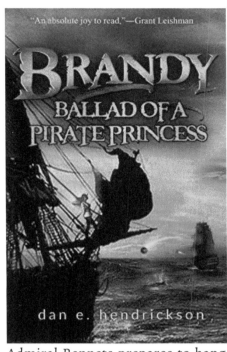

"An absolute joy to read."—Grant Leishman

Brandy, Ballad of a Pirate Princess by Dan E. Hendrickson is about a girl raised by pirates. Brandy's mother is the hot-tempered Scarlet Mistress, and her father is Captain Eric Erasmus, better known as "The Plague." Both of Brandy's parents have been pirates since before her birth on the Red Witch 15 years ago. First mate, Don Lomoche, kills Captain Erasmus after notifying Admiral Bennets of the Navy Fleet who the Scarlet Mistress is.

Her mother's real name was Katrina Mooney; she had killed her master after being sold into slavery when she was 13 years old. Her master was King George's cousin, and she has been on the run from execution ever since.

Admiral Bennets prepares to hang her onboard her ship, but before he can, she curses the crew by telling them only her heir can release them from the Red Witch curse, flings herself overboard, and hangs herself. Brandy and her Uncle Skinner disguise themselves to blend in with the prisoners below deck and are taken to Jamaica as enslaved people. Before her death, Brandy's mother tells her she has two choices: reclaim Red Witch or live on land. Admiral Bennets gives Don Lomoche ownership of the Red Witch. What life does Brandy choose? Does she rightfully take back the Red Witch?

I like many things about this book. Firstly, the author uses subheadings that helped me understand the distance traveled between locations. Secondly, the author provides vivid descriptions of the events on the Caribbean islands and the sea. I could easily imagine the pirate battles on the ships, the enslaved people fleeing for safety, and ships cresting huge waves during hurricanes. Thirdly, the book was full of suspense and kept me guessing how it would end. Finally, there are a few lessons to learn in this book. Some of my favorites are that free men work harder when they earn something they can appreciate and enjoy, love is more powerful than hate, and the reality of fate is that it can be both kind and cruel.

There was nothing I disliked about this book. I had to appreciate that pirates do not know how to speak or think using correct grammar. I continually had to stop myself from wanting to count errors that were not actual errors. When incorrect grammar was not in dialogue, I had to pay close attention to whom the thought processes belonged. This book is fast-paced and action-packed, with battles and love mingled throughout the plot.

The author has done a great job writing this book and keeping the plot flowing from page to page. The book appears to have been edited by a professional editor, as I only found two minor errors in the entire book. For these reasons, I gladly give this book 4 out of 4 stars.

I recommend this book to readers who enjoy historical fiction about pirates.

# The Prodigy Slave, Book One: Journey to Winter Garden

## Londyn Skye

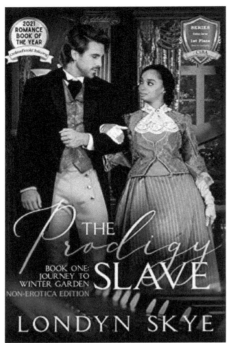

Maya was confident that her master would never sell her daughter because he was the one who named the child Lily. As the years went by, a terrible nightmare was the next journey of her beloved daughter. Lily never forgot her chaotic experiences with her father that kept torturing her mind.

She lives many miles away from her mother and never knows if she's still alive. One thing that gives her a soothing calmness is only playing the piano, a forbidden act of an enslaved person. She learns music by only listening to the piano keys while sneaking out to watch Mrs Elizabeth Adams teaching piano lessons. Jesse Adams isn't as bad as the other enslaver, but he would never spare a rod into countless lash if he knew the enslaved people disobeyed him. Unfortunately, James, the son of Lily's master, discovers her secret talent. Unbeknownst to him, Lily had been fond of him since they were young. They were friends back then. Will this man become a culprit of Lily's demise, or will he remain standing on Lily's side, despite the Slave Code, for their friendship?

The Prodigy Slave, Book One: Journey to Winter Garden by Londyn Skye, is a beautiful romance novel featuring an enslaved person and her possessor. I didn't even know that a Slave Code ever existed until I chose to read this novel. The code gave me an idea of why racial conflicts are still at the onset of the 21st century; and made me curious how an enslaved person with a pleasant talent excelled in a forbidden time. I liked the narrative in each chapter because it looked like a dramatized version of the code. Can you imagine a woman of color having an outstanding accomplishment beyond the Slave Code Law in their time? Moreover, the enslavers' character buildup seemed true to their position, especially in their rage or angry outbursts. The scenes with them took away dull moments, which I appreciated the most.

On the other hand, I found the dialogue struggling. The slang language in this novel was the thing I liked the least. I also stammered while reading about the characters' conversation, making me slow down. In between the switching of dialogues and monologue, I also needed clarification. In addition to my least favorite, I tried to find a song's composition, but I only saw simple lyrics beyond the glorious description of Lily's character.

I rate this book 4 out of 4 stars because the Slave Codes amazed me. The code exposed that people of color suffered from inhumane activities.

Furthermore, this novel contained explicit scenes, and those scenarios were not good for a person below eighteen years old.

# Chameleons

## Onyx Gold

Zia is the first to welcome Bryce when she meets him in the Fargo Tower elevator on the first day of his new job as an investment attorney. Bryce fills Zia's office with red roses and leaves a note asking her to dinner. He has a $20,000 Marchesa black gown, a pair of $4,000 shoes, and Cartier diamond heart-motif earrings delivered to her. Although they are attracted to each other, the date is a disaster. She receives a copy of a crime thriller manuscript in her email from Baxter Leopold. She loves the manuscript and offers Baxter a partnership, and her friend, Sasha, agrees to publish the book. Baxter wants Zia to meet with him in New York and offers her an all-expense-paid trip. In the meantime, women's body parts are being found in the Hudson River and Long Island Sound. Is it safe for Zia to go to New York? Do Zia and Bryce have a chance at romance?

Read Chameleons by Onyx Gold to find out. My favorite aspect of this action-packed book is the lessons this book provides. For instance, the book stresses that people you meet online can be whoever and whatever they want to be, and this can be dangerous because you will not know the difference until you meet them in person, when it could be too late. Onyx Gold also points out that you should never judge others' reactions to certain events because you do not know how you will react in the same situation. The author has done an excellent job with character development, and I felt like I knew each character personally. My favorite character was Jazz, the best understanding and nonjudgmental friend everyone should have. Some of the author's descriptions, like "hurt feelings feel like venomous scorpion stings," made me laugh out loud.

I found nothing to dislike in this well-written book. The plot is fast-paced and flows smoothly. Some of the content is gory, but that is not unusual in a crime thriller, so I do not consider it a flaw.

This book appears to have been edited by a professional editor, as I only found a handful of errors in the entire book. I have no reason not to give this book 4 out of 4 stars.

I recommend this book to mature adult readers only because of the erotic sexual content, the gory murder scenes, and the non-borderline profanity. This content may make sensitive readers want to avoid this book.

# WatchDogs Abnormal Beginnings

## Mike L Junior

WatchDogs: Abnormal Beginnings is a fiction book written by Mike L. Junior. Once upon a time on a planet, a disaster befell a whole nation. Dr. Drake Nathan manufactures a chip that could do lots of things such as regulate blood pressure, metabolism, and cholesterol and also treat cancer patients. This invention paved a way for other inventions and this brought about advanced technology. Many years after, people started dying in great numbers because development ceased considering that Drake's invention stopped working. Scientists found a way and moved the remaining people alive to a different planet. Many people started passing out as a result of toxic air, while few weren't affected by it. The immune people relocated to Georgia and thereafter split into five nations.

Among these few, another minor set of people with special abilities emerged. Read this story to find out how these abnormal people were discriminated against and how they pulled through the situation. I love how the part of this book that described how the researchers worked hard to find solutions to the death of the people caused by the toxic air they were breathing was portrayed. The researchers finally invented a machine that could help people with artificial oxygen. In real life, this scene shows that research is very important for the progress and development of a nation, considering that research is all about solving problems. In addition, when situations overwhelm people, they usually question the essence of their religion and, most times, stop believing in their God. Only a few whose faith is firm can hold fast to their belief. The strategy that befell these people that experienced the apocalypse made many of them become atheists. Indeed, a stable nation brings peace and mental stability to people.

I learned from this book that when things are not working well even after we've tried to make it work, by all means, tackling the problem using a different approach can help solve it or lighten the issue. Leaving the situation the way it is without trying again to solve it would only worsen it. When the scientist sensed that the toxic air would consume the remaining people on the earth, they took proactive steps immediately by moving the people into five different nations, namely, DcOnious, Dadrak, Lorenzia, Xenora, and Yazar. This division approach truly saved many lives.

I will excitedly rate this book 4 out of 4 stars because I wouldn't say I liked no part of it. The author's book was professionally edited, considering that only a few errors were discovered. The characters that made up this story played their roles perfectly well, making each chapter more interesting.

Do fictional thrillers appeal to you? Do you enjoy books whose content focuses on searching for a missing treasure? Does technology intrigue you? Do you desire to know how teamwork helped in solving this crisis? If the answer is yes, I recommend this book to you because the content suits your interest.

# Wild World
## Peter S. Rush

The National Guard opened fire on students, killing four and leaving nine others wounded during a peaceful demonstration against the Vietnam War at Kent State University. After listening to Sergeant Durk, Steve Logan accepts that changing the system from the inside is the best path toward reformation. Most of his friends are against the idea of him dropping his ambition to get into law school to join the Providence Police Department; his girlfriend, Roxy Fisher, supports him. As is often the case in life, change takes time, and some will resist it vehemently.

Wild World is a historical fiction authored by Peter S. Rush. The development of the characters was brilliant; I enjoyed being introduced to strangers, getting to know them, and rooting for some in the fullness of time. It made the reading experience more enthralling. Steve enters a fight. He does not know what it will cost him, but he never gives up. Additionally, he is paired with different experienced officers who not only demonstrate the condition of the force but also serve to highlight his traits. One will realize and appreciate that doing the right thing is costly.

Will Steve overcome the alluring feeling that accompanies power from acting as the judge and jury? It is always exciting to walk down memory lane, particularly when you have an author who knows how to delicately and intricately throw in factual events in a fictional narrative. Peter introduces several themes prevalent in the mid-nineteenth century, including the protests against the war and the women's rights movement, making the book entertaining and enlightening. Overall, every aspect of Wild World was excellent; I disliked nothing about it.

Every reader that picks this book will love the thrill of trying to uncover how deep the rot runs. Steve underestimated the impact of jumping into unknown waters. One can only hope that it is not bottomless. As the story progresses, one witnesses the consequences of Steve's decision and the dilemma he battles as the war rages on. I had to keep on reading to know the outcome and how those around Steve would be affected.

I rate the book 4 out of 4 stars and heartily recommend it to ardent readers of historical fiction. While there are no horses and violent outlaws that characterize the Wild West, the numerous cases Steve has to handle and his fight against systemic corruption make this world wild. The story is a reminder that change does not come by itself and that dogged determination is an essential ingredient when introducing reform. Equally, it recognizes the role of law enforcement officers while disclosing the possibility of abusing the powers given to this critical office.

# When No One Else Believed

## Ron Tripodo

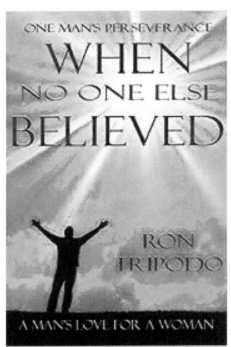

When No One Else Believed is a non-fictional work written by Ron Tripodo. In this book, the author narrates a troubling part of his life growing up with ADHD, his wife's illness, and his journey to build unwavering faith in God.

The author, Ron, begins this book by narrating part of his life growing up. He had ADHD when the disorder had not been known and a treatment developed; this impaired his learning and attention capabilities. He lived with this for a very long time; however, I was surprised at how he made a living for himself. Next, he moves on to the next part of the book, The Miracle, where he narrates how his wife, Patsy, caught a dangerous and rare illness, Herpes Simplex Encephalitis (HSE), which had a high mortality rate. He also gives readers a brief history of their love story, how they met, some of the problems they faced, and how they overcame them. Read this book to know if Patsy survives her illness. How does Ron's faith play into this? I had a good time reading this book. I was amazed at the severity of Ron's faith, even in the most difficult of situations; as a Christian, this was something I admired. Tripodo tells this story from a first-person narrative, which actively engages readers at every turn as events unfold. They can feel the myriad of emotions running through the author's mind while writing the story. The love Patsy and Ron shared was admirable; it radiated a pure and selfless form that could be rare to find. I also felt sorry for Patsy at a point; it could not have been easy for her. The little picture inserts the author included added credibility and emotion to the story.

There was nothing I disliked about this story. Its plot, presentation, and narration were top-notch. My emotions were on a ride throughout the story; sometimes, I was glad, and other times I felt sorry for Ron, especially when his workers at home all thought he was going crazy. I only encountered a minor error while reading this piece.

I rate this book 4 out of 4 stars for the positive aspects listed above. I appreciated that this author was not afraid to pinpoint his weaknesses; I believe this makes him strong. His faith was another thing I enjoyed; it was strong. I recommend this book to people interested in non-fiction and inspirational genres. People who want to develop their faith can also read this.

# Blue Collar Cash: Love Your Work Secure Your Future Find Happiness for Life
## Ken Rusk

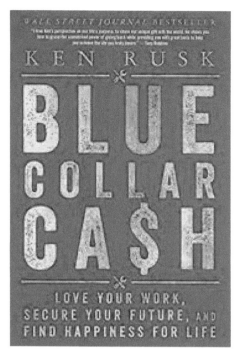

Ken Rusk's non-fiction book, Blue Collar Cash, delves into the subject of successful blue-collar careers. Rusk is a successful business owner who worked many blue-collar jobs before starting his lucrative construction business. Rusk wants to help readers realize they may have a future in the trades. The author outlines multiple character traits identified with successful blue-collar workers and entrepreneurs. This book follows the stories of many of Rusk's friends and employees who have discovered the ability to find comfort, peace, and financial freedom.

I appreciate the author's focus on comfort, peace, and financial freedom. Rusk refers to these three qualities throughout the book and shows the reader how to design a life to achieve them.

One might think from the title that cash is the primary driver of success. However, without happiness, money means nothing. Additionally, the author emphasizes that he is not "anti-college." Rusk recognizes that some crucial careers require additional education. Instead, he argues that college should not be the standard, especially for people unsure of their career path when embarking on their college career. Rusk states that readers should envision their future and build career choices to achieve that dream.

There was nothing I disliked about this book. The author's assessment of choosing a college degree or a blue-collar trade is correct. I have seen too many young people attend college and incur massive debt with no vision of their future. Before starting this book, I thought I would disagree with the author on many points. However, Rusk proved me wrong and taught me valuable lessons about designing my life to suit my needs instead of living around my work. This book is for every person of working age.

I rate Blue Collar Cash 4 out of 4 stars. Although I am not in a blue-collar career and am not actively considering a switch from healthcare, I found many applicable discussions in this book. The author argues that people can develop successful and lucrative careers without college. I appreciate the author backing up his discussion points with specific research, and he often plays devil's advocate by considering the other side of his argument. I found only one minor error in this well-edited book, which did not impact my rating.

I recommend this book to readers who are considering their future careers. Young people who are told to go to college but are uncertain about their career paths can discover a love for the blue-collar lifestyle after reading this non-fiction book. College is not the only road to success. Rusk outlines a variety of blue-collar careers that can lead to financial freedom for readers. Although this book applies to all age groups, the author discusses the desire to reach young people before they go to college.

# Totem: (Strong Heart, #3)

## Charlie Sheldon

Totem by Charlie Sheldon is the third book in the Strong Heart Series. Written about the indigenous peoples of the Pacific Northwest, this series weaves tales around the past and present. Preceded by Strong Heart and Adrift, this final installment finishes the story perfectly.

Sarah Cooley lives with her grandfather, Tom-Tom. They plan to hike in Bear Valley with their family and friends. When something happens to interrupt the plan, things look hopeless. In addition, mysterious elk-kills seem to keep happening at the wildlife refuge. Carl Larsen's investigations haven't turned up much so far. Whatever is going on, it's all happening in Bear Valley. It would only take one artifact found in the valley to save the entire area from the imminent mining operation. Will the secrets of Bear Valley be revealed? You'll have to read the book to find out! I loved the continuous element of suspense that pervades this tale. The way that each set of characters finds their way toward Bear Valley keeps the pace quick without leaving readers behind. Although there were some unexpected surprises for me in this novel, I cannot divulge any secrets here. Suffice it to say, this book provides another great addition, and finale, to this three-volume series. This book has a lot of great features. It is divided into two books or parts that help with the elements of the story. The characters take us through a type of pilgrimage through the history of the Pacific Northwest and its culture. The tale draws a reader to ask interesting questions about history. How did the indigenous peoples of the past deal with climate change in their time? How would one prepare for climate warming or cooling? The answers may surprise you. I was fascinated by the concepts touched upon in this story that could apply to present-day situations. This adventure is immersive, and losing yourself in the pages is easy. However, with the handy maps provided at the beginning of this novel, you're sure to navigate your way back out again!

I have always been impressed by this author's ability to create characters that are larger than life. Each one's characteristics become so familiar that the reader could recognize them on the street were they real. Sarah is an excellent example of a 14-year-old with an attitude that one could take as stubborn. In truth, she shows a strength of character and a love for life.

This author also shows a well-researched scientific background regarding the mining and northwest history that make up the foundation of this story. Steeped in history, one of the best things about this tale is how it advocates keeping traditions alive in an ever-changing world. I found that to be one of the most important messages of the book.

I found no negatives to list for this book. It is exceptionally well-edited. I highly recommend this novel to readers that enjoy adventure and discovery. It will appeal to those who like learning about ancient northern cultures. This book is more than suitable for a young adult audience as profanity is brief and mild, and although there are a few violent scenes, they are short. This series will admirably grace the bookshelves of homes and libraries. I rate Totem with a shining 4 out of 4 stars for these reasons!

# AUTHOR INTERVIEW

## ZONA: THE FORBIDDEN LAND
## FRED G. BAKER

*Let's have a chat*

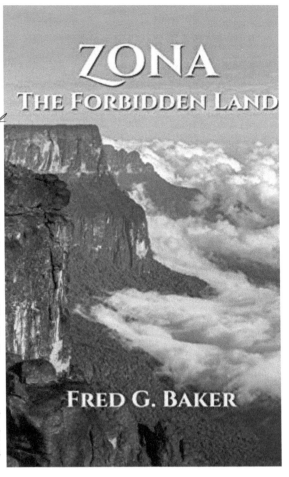

### When did you first realize you wanted to be a writer?

I always enjoyed listening to and telling stories when young. In high school, I wrote my first short stories. After a career in science and engineering, where I wrote many reports and papers, I learned to write clearly and accurately. Later, I tried my hand at biographies and fiction. It is much fun to be free to invent a story and world.

### What would you say is your interesting writing quirk?

I think about my story and draft parts of it, scenes sometimes until they seem to work, then I work out details in my dreams. I don't know how many people dream of their stories, but I do to some extent.

### As a child, what did you want to do when you grew up?

I always wanted to be a scientist and work in a lab with lots of shiny glass equipment like condensers and flasks. Lots of bubbling colorful liquids. I studied geology, computing, physics, and engineering in college, so it helped me with science-based plots.

### What was one of the most surprising things you learned in creating your book?

I always enjoy learning the history and culture of the areas that I include in my stories. Most of my books draw heavily from my own travel, living experience, and people that I've met. It's easier to write and be authentic if you have firsthand experience with the role of the character or his environs.

### Where did you get your information or idea for your book?

The ideas come from observing everyday life or when I am relaxed on vacation. For instance, my novel The Black Freighter is based on observations while on vacation on the island of Grenada, where I witnessed some aspects of the story and the local culture. I was there during a hotly contested national election, and so I wrote some of that energy and activity into the story.

# NIGHTLORD: SUNSET
# GARON WHITED

### When did you first realize you wanted to be a writer?

My first clue was when I started playing D&D, way back in the dim and misty past. There were stories to be told and I didn't always have people to tell them with. It can be hard to get a group together to play. But if I'm writing, all I need is something to write on. Stories are always there, waiting, whether they're made with other people or with pen and ink. It's only a matter of how you tell them. One is collaborative, adapting to how others tell stories—and the story they want to tell—while the other is entirely yours, your story, your rules, your ideas.

### How do you schedule your life when you're writing?

It's pretty simple, actually. I wake up, make a grueling commute to my office—ten, twelve steps, thereabouts—sit down, fire up the computer, and write. At some point, I notice I'm hungry, so I eat. During breaks, I do other little things. Laundry. Mail.Yard work. Dishes. Then I write stuff some more. Eventually, I made more typos than real words. That's my cue to go to bed, whenever that happens to be. I sleep until I wake up, and I repeat the process until I have a novel. Then I start a new novel. Although, once in a while, I'll take a break between books and think about other books.

### What do you like to do when you're not writing?

If for some reason, I'm not writing, my usual preference is to sit around a table with half a dozen other people and play role-playing games. If that's not feasible, I'll read. I usually go for the game, mostly because it's more seldom. Getting people together to play is far more difficult than reading. The books are always there. They don't have schedules or jobs or appointments. I can wake up wondering where I recall a phrase from, and the books are willing to help, no matter the hour. Getting people together to play is rare, so I grab the opportunity whenever it presents itself.

### What was one of the most surprising thing you learned in creating your book?

Typos are alive. They creep into the binding of the book and lay eggs. Later, after publication, the eggs hatch and slither into the text. No matter what you do—spell check, editors, rewrites—the sneaky little things always reappear. It's easy to see them, too. I generally find a typo nest in the binding when I get my author copy of a book. I flip it open to some random page, and there it is, a typo, blatant as a bug on a windshield. They annoy me, but I've learned to be more philosophical about them. It's a process, and it might take the rest of my life.

# PROJECT TAU
# JUDE AUSTIN

## As a child, what did you want to do when you grew up?

Everything! I was impressionable as warm wax when I was a kid. When I went to the dentist, I'd come back wanting to be a dentist. When I got my hair cut, I was determined to be a hairdresser. Ironically, the one job I never actively considered was writing! Writing had always been a part of my life, so it was never something I decided to try so much as something I'd always done. It didn't occur to me to try and make a living from it until much, much later.

## How did you get your book published?

Amazon KDP. I'd previously dismissed it as an avenue, since it wasn't an option when I started (although Project Tau was published in 2016, it was written about ten years earlier). One day, I just thought, "Why not?" I converted my manuscript to Kindle format and got a cover designed. The first cover was appalling, so I replaced it as soon as I was able, and it went from there. I'm aiming at becoming a hybrid author in the future and will be seeking representation for my brand-new fantasy series.

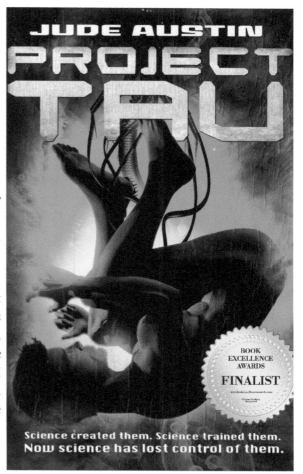

Science created them. Science trained them. Now science has lost control of them.

## Where did you get your information or idea for your book?

I never plan my books, so it's not really a case of, "I think this idea would make a great story." In all cases, I start writing, and the story grows as I watch. The real inspiration for Project Tau was that I'd just finished writing a novel of the "epic journey across an alien planet" variety. I wanted to try writing a story set in a very small area. The nice thing about sci-fi realism is that it ignores science in favor of character and world development, so I didn't need much scientific knowledge.

## What was one of the most surprising things you learned in creating your book?

I don't remember anything like that while I was writing it, but there was something that happened when it was Book of the Month on Online Book Club. As Project Tau deals so much with human rights, a few lively debates were going on about what the future of cloning might look like. What surprised me – and shocked me a little, if I'm honest! – was that there were quite a few people who came down on the villain's side, saying that clones should be considered fair game for any treatment, no matter how brutal, simply because they're clones.

# PILOT WHO KNOWS THE WATERS
# N.L. HOLMES

### When did you first realize you wanted to be a writer?

I've always loved books, and I come from a family where writing isn't an impossible career choice: my aunt was book editor of the local paper, and my father wrote short stories for Boys Life. A cousin had written a book. I wrote "novels" as a kid just for fun, but I really had my heart set on archaeology from an early age. I ended up teaching, although I wrote academic things. Eventually, as I approached retirement from the classroom, I decided writing novels would be a great way to use my interest in and knowledge of the deep past.

### What would you say is your interesting writing quirk?

I'm a "pantser"; that is, I write by the seat of my pants rather than planning much in advance. In many of my novels, I've had an idea of specific scenes I wanted to include well before I knew the overarching plot in detail. So, I write those scenes first, out of order. Afterward, I can put them in order—that becomes my "outline"-- and weave them together.

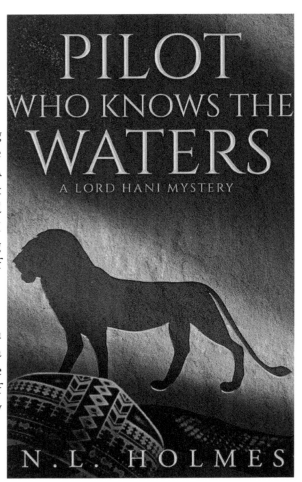

### Where did you get your information or idea for your book?

All my books are based on real events, some following known history more closely and others just borrowing the setting and historical moment. The Lord Hani Mysteries take place in and after the reign of Akhenaten, the Heretic Pharaoh. We're lucky enough to have many of the diplomatic correspondences of his reign that describe actual missions of Hani! Then, I fatten those events up and throw in a murder mystery and a family drama.

### What do you like to do when you're not writing?

I have too many interests! I like to weave, garden, play the violin, dance, and hike. Lately, I've gotten into genealogy, and the fall season is busy with canning and drying the summer crops. And then, poetry has once again become a passion after forty years of absence, both in reading (I belong to a "contemporary poetry book club") and in producing. But I guess that counts as writing.

### What was one of the most surprising thing you learned in creating your book?

In doing research for the latest Lord Hani mystery, I discovered that lions and leopards lived all over the eastern Mediterranean, including Turkey and Greece. There were even elephants in Syria. We've really impoverished the fauna of our planet, not to mention stripping the forest that once covered all the same area.

# THE MAESTRO MONOLOGUE
# ROB WHITE

### How do you schedule your life when you're writing?

My life is all about writing. The appropriate question for me would be: "What's your schedule when you're not writing?" The answer would be, "Schedule in more time to write."

### What would you say is your interesting writing quirk?

I will wake up, in the middle of the night, with the idea that I have to immediately put on paper, or I cannot fall back to sleep.

### Where did you get your information or idea for your book?

My ideas pretty much come from my life experiences, exclusively.

### How do you process and deal with negative book reviews?

I love them. They teach me how to see possibilities, in my writing, that I could not see.

### Is there anything you would like to confess about as an author?

I am inspiringly addicted and wonderfully obsessed with writing, so much so that I can forget to eat.

# THE FREEDOM BUILDING
# MARTIN KENDALL

### What do you like to do when you're not writing?

I like listening to, and playing, the piano. My favorite composer is J. S. Bach because he combines both the emotional and intellectual faculties of the human experience like no other artist.

### What was one of the most surprising thing you learned in creating your book?

I was surprised to learn how one or two paragraphs early on in the book can set the tone for the entire novel, particularly in regard to character and plot development. If a person is said to be uptight, for instance, this might mean something deeper is at play, which might have a significant role in the plot. One, or two, character personas, especially in regard to writing psychological thrillers, can have great significance in the story.

### As a child, what did you want to do when you grew up?

I wanted to train in an elite fighting unit. I wanted to have martial skills and weapons skills like Rambo. I wanted to jump from aeroplanes, swim in seas, and battle evil people in the pursuit of truth and justice.

His building...
his genius...
his darkness.

### Is there anything you would like to confess about as an author?

If somebody disturbs me whilst I am writing, I can become grumpy. The world I pictured is shattered in an instant, and it takes a while to return to it. My long-suffering girlfriend knows this and, unless the house is burning down, knows not to disturb me.

### How do you process and deal with negative book reviews?

I love extreme reviews that are either very negative or very positive. If my book has evoked an extreme opinion, then I feel I have done my job as a writer. The worst book reviews are simply ordinary.

# THE SWORD SWALLOWER AND A CHICO KID
# GARY ROBINSON

### When did you first realize you wanted to be a writer?

I remember in the 2nd grade when the teacher allowed us an hour of 'free time.' So, I would find a scrap piece of paper and write a short story that always started with the words, "Once upon a time."

### How do you schedule your life when you're writing?

Every aspect of my life becomes inconvenient when I am writing. That includes using the restroom.

### What would you say is your interesting writing quirk?

I will stop in mid-sentence if I feel I am writing simply to complete the sentence. I want every word and every sentence to be part of an elaborate artistic exercise.

### Where did you get your information or idea for your book?

My book, "The Sword Swallower and a Chico Kid," was inspired by my friendship with Captain Don Leslie.

### As a child, what did you want to do when you grew up?

Everything from author to baseball player.

### What do you like to do when you're not writing?

I love to play harmonica. The locals in my town who do not know me personally but have seen me play call me the harmonica man. I also spend a lot of time listening and formulating content while consuming adult beverages.

### What was one of the most surprising things you learned in creating your book?

The most surprising part of producing my first novel was reading the glowing reviews outlining the quality of the story and my abilities as a writer. I also discovered how little I understand our complex language.

### Is there anything you would like to confess about as an author?

I have promised the universe to elevate the human condition through entertaining narratives.

### How do you process and deal with negative book reviews?

I take each review as a message from the universe. I look for patterns in my reviews and adjust accordingly.

# EAST WIND, 2ND EDITION
# JACK WINNICK

### When did you first realize you wanted to be a writer?

I have been writing as part of my professional work as a Professor of Chemical Engineering and Engineering Consultant since graduating from college many years ago. This eventually led to the writing of fiction as my knowledge of the Middle East has grown over the years.

### How did you get your first book published?

I found a publisher in the available literature who was willing to read my first book and liked it.

### Where did you get your information or idea for your book?

Mainly open literature (never Wikipedia; stay away from that source!). But also from governmental agencies as part of my work for the U.S. State Department.

### What do you like to do when you're not writing?

Playing tennis; watching foreign films, especially British, French, and Scandinavian. I frankly have given up on Hollywood productions. Of course, if an offer came along…

### How do you process and deal with negative book reviews?

I have, fortunately, received very few legitimate negative reviews. Constructive ones I use to help edit the story. The irrational ones I don't bother with. Life's too short to bother with idiots.

# FINAL NOTICE
## VAN FLEISHER

### When did you first realize you wanted to be a writer?

I'd written several short stories and found the process interesting, and then my cousin wrote a historical fiction novel. (Gone for a Soldier by Jeffry Hepple). That was probably the seed, but it was twenty years later that I started writing a book, and then another 17 years passed before I wrote one.

### How do you schedule your life when you're writing?

My life – even in retirement – is very busy, so the question is, really, "How do I schedule my writing?" I don't write to deadlines. Writing is my hobby, so I write when I feel like it and I have enough time to focus.

### What would you say is your interesting writing quirk?

I'm not very good when it comes to grammar. I tend to write the same way that I speak, so I tend to "comma-tize" phrases. Drives my editor and some comma-nazi readers nuts.

### How did you get your book published?

I used BookBaby for my first book and then completely self-published for books two and three.

### Where did you get your information or idea for your book?

Combination of the news and my interests. For example, I'd been a distance runner for much of my life, and the expanding sports watch technology intrigued me. I imagined a day when the watches would tell you when you're going to die. Then, with all the guns available, I imagined people using their guns because they knew they were dying soon.

# EDITOR'S PICK

## A DREAM FOR PEACE: AN AMBASSADOR MEMOIR BY DR. GHOULEM BERRAH

A Dream for Peace is the most captivating Ambassador's Memoir. Young Ghoulem Berrah was a Freedom Fighter for the Independence of Algeria. While an activist medical student in Bordeaux, France, he fled the country to enroll in the Algerian war. His Excellency Dr. Ghoulem Berrah (1938-2011) was a tireless proponent of world peace. After President Siad Barre of Somalia, took the port of Berbera from the Russians, Dr. Berrah was charged with delivering the news to the American President Jimmy Carter. In the middle of the diplomatic imbroglios, the author unfolds the chronicle of a fascinating love story. A devout Muslim and interfaith Leader, he walks with you through Mecca, the Vatican, and Jerusalem. A compelling story for any reader.

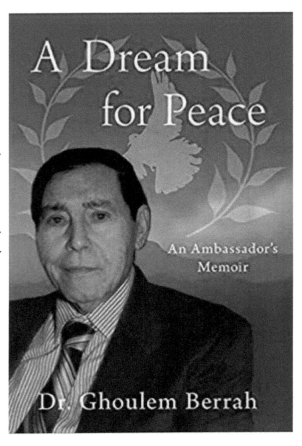

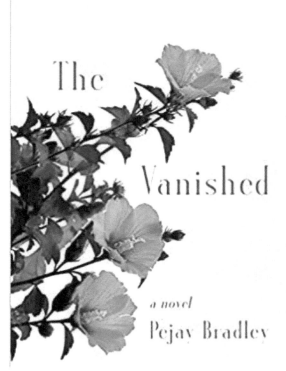

## THE VANISHED BY PEJAY BRADLEY

The way of life and the culture in this story once existed and since have vanished; a new country and a different society have emerged from the old Korea. The turbulent years of this transformation swept many individuals and families into complete destruction. Some are still remembered, while others disappeared from all accounts. Embon, born into a aristocratic family during the Japanese occupation of Korea, is thrown into jail for nationalistic activities. Released after coming down with tuberculosis, he decides to join his former classmates in Shanghai to work for the banned Korean Provisional Government. Although he is not yet fully recovered from his illness, he joins the fight and witnesses the violent deaths of his friends and other young Koreans during their pursuit of Korean independence from Japan.

Lightning Source UK Ltd.
Milton Keynes UK
UKHW050623150123
415184UK00005B/1